D1647523

IT'S QU

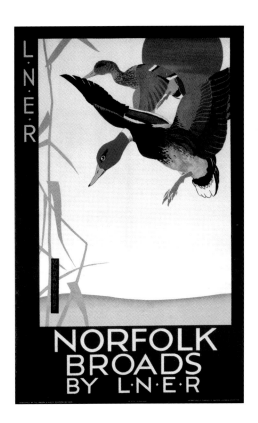

L·N·E·R

NORFOLK
BROADS
BY L·N·E·R

Beverley Cole

Capital Transport

LNER Poster 1935. The Silver Forth by Norman Wilkinson.

ISBN 185414 304 2
Published in association with the National Railway Museum by Capital Transport Publishing, PO Box 250, Harrow, HA3 5ZH
© Capital Transport Publishing and NRM 2006

Introduction

'Its Quicker By Rail' is probably the most memorable catchphrase coined by the LNER advertising department but there was much more to their sophisticated advertising strategy than catchphrases …

On December 31st 1922 the hundred-plus railway companies of this country were grouped together into four concerns; the London & North Eastern Railway, the London Midland & Scottish Railway, the Great Western Railway, and the Southern Railway. The territory of the new LNER, incorporating the old NER, stretched from King's Cross up to Scotland on the east side of the country. In 1924 the *LNER Magazine* boasted that their latest poster was "notable as being the first reproduction of a design for which a Royal Academician has been commissioned by a railway company. It is by Frank Brangwyn. RA, who actually executed the drawing and tinting on the stone from which the copies were taken by the auto-litho process". The LMS was also using Royal Academicians to design its posters in 1924, so the LNER claim may not be quite so outstanding as it appears and Frank Brangwyn had in fact designed a poster for a shipping company about twenty years earlier.

Whatever the facts there is no doubt that W. M. Teasdale recognised the need for a high standard of design in the LNER posters but he chose artists with more progressive styles rather than the traditional type of Academician. Amongst the artists he commissioned, Austin Cooper, Frank Newbould, Tom Purvis, Fred Taylor and Frank Mason have become known as the 'big five'. To these must be added the names of R. E. Higgins, Andrew Johnson and Graham Simmons, amongst many others, who contributed some outstanding designs to the LNER Publicity Department.

The LNER suffered few of the early conflicts that troubled the Southern and LMS. Relations between the constituent companies were generally amicable and the new company soon got into its stride. In February 1923 it appointed William Teasdale as its Advertising Manager. Teasdale had been Trade Advertising Agent with the North Eastern Railway, a company that had set high standards in its poster work and methods of display, and he had definite views on the role of the advertising man. Good relationships with colleagues were important, but the advertising man had to have complete charge of all advertising.

Its first poster, issued in March 1923, featured a view by Fred Taylor of the interior of York Minster. It was much admired. "One of the finest coloured posters ever issued in connection with railway publicity," commented the Railway Gazette; "if it may be regarded as a criterion of the posters to come from the same quarter. It may confidently be set down as a happy augury" (16 March 1923). It

was, and over the next few months a stream of colourful images appeared on the hoardings as the campaign initiated by Teasdale began to get under way. The designs that he commissioned stretched to all corners of the system. Posters of resorts were most numerous and covered the East Coast from Southend as far north as Dunbar. Inland and continental attractions were well represented, and Frank Mason contributed a study of dock facilities at Blyth. There was also an example of what was later to be referred to as 'reminder advertising' featuring a woodcut of the Flying Scotsman by H L Oakley with the title 'Travel to Scotland by the East Coast Route'. Reminder advertising was used by the LNER to provide a constant reminder to passengers about its major routes. Slogans such as 'King's Cross for Scotland' and 'Harwich for the Continent' were to appear frequently on posters and other publicity material.

In December 1926 Teasdale took the unusual step of offering contracts to five artists if they would agree not to work for any of the other three railway companies. Austin Cooper, Frank Mason, Frank Newbould, Tom Purvis and Fred Taylor had all been working for the LNER for some time, and Teasdale guaranteed to commission posters from each artist for the three years to the end of 1929. He made it clear that the contracts would make no difference to the relationship between company and artist and that they might not like some of the subjects they were asked to do. All five accepted, with Taylor guaranteed the highest sum of £1,000.

The scheme was a great success. The LNER had not only ensured that the core of their poster work was of a consistently high standard, but also that the artists were not able to work for any of their rivals. Taylor was the most popular of the five, and his architectural studies in particular were always much admired, but it was Purvis who received the most critical acclaim both for his boldness and originality. "He understands the value of elimination" wrote a reviewer in *The Observer* on 17 March 1929 "and of reducing every subject to its simplest forms, and bare essentials. His effective flat patterns explain themselves in a flash."

The LNER also moved towards greater standardisation in its poster designs during these years. Greater attention was also paid to display. The LNER, together with the other railway companies, produced most of its posters in either quad royal or double royal size. Posters for public hoardings were produced in 16 sheet size and the LNER also made use of long 'streamers' which were never less than 100 x 42 in. Hoardings were coded so that posters could be easily sited for best effect and did not get lost among other advertisements. Displays of the work of particular artists were frequently staged at larger stations.

During the 1930s posters increasingly stressed the comfort of rail travel. Dining whilst travelling was not unusual, and the more prestigious trains boasted all-electric kitchens with both set and à la carte menus. The wine list on such trains as the *West Riding Limited*, the *Coronation* and the *Flying Scotsman* would not disgrace a restaurant today. In 1938 the *West Riding Limited* offered no fewer than five different kinds of champagne and nine brands of mineral water!

Some of the best advertising of these years was used to promote trains and services. Many of the companies had stressed the speed and comfort of their trains, particularly those that operated the lines between London and Scotland. This rivalry was pursued by the LMS and LNER during the 1920s. Both the *Royal Scot* of the LMS and *Flying Scotsman* of the LNER ran non-stop to Scotland but they did not compete on speed; it was not until the following decade that the pace began to quicken. In 1935 the LNER introduced its first streamlined train, the *Silver Jubilee*, which ran between London and Newcastle. This was followed two years later by the *Coronation* which covered the distance between London and Edinburgh in only 6 hours. The LMS hit back with the *Coronation Scot* which took an extra thirty minutes between London and Glasgow.

These trains, with their own locomotives and carriages were highly distinctive and extremely popular. They generated an enormous amount of publicity material, including many posters. Frank Mason, Tom Purvis and Doris Zinkeisen all produced designs for the *Coronation*. Although speed was important it was not seen as the only way of attracting passengers, and both the LMS and LNER emphasised the standard of comfort and facilities available on these and other trains. The *Flying Scotsman* boasted a hairdressing saloon, ladies' resting room, Louis XVI Restaurant and cocktail bar and even a cinema coach for a short period. Several posters were issued by the LNER to advertise its restaurant car and dining facilities, including work by Tom Purvis and A R Thomson, as well as the 'Chef and Waiter' series by Austin Cooper.

The North Eastern Railway Company had been particularly enthusiastic in its use of pictorial posters to advertise its health and holiday resorts and some of its posters were considered to be the finest examples of Edwardian poster advertising.

In 1912 E. M. Horsley, Advertising Manager of the NER, gave a lecture in which he divided railway advertising into five groups including "hoarding advertisements, the principal considerations being (a) attractiveness and (b) position". In the previous year it had been suggested to the NER that railway poster hoardings should be numbered and organised so that there was no conflict of interest between the commercial advertisers and the railway company. This was adopted and further refined so that some sites were recognised as being of greater value than others.

Horsley also remarked that station advertising was most useful "because the bills (or posters) were before the people who had nothing better to do than study them". He also appealed to the company's staff for ideas for the posters as it was increasingly difficult to find new subjects, and suggestions were warmly welcomed.

In 1914, in an article entitled 'Railways and Art', A. E. Wiseman of the York District Goods Office indicated the current state of advertising – "Railway companies are keenly alive to the value and necessity for advertising their wares in as attractive and alluring manner as possible. To do this effectively they have recourse to art. Large sums are spent annually in gorgeous posters and highly finished photographs to induce the travelling public to patronise the beauty spots and health resorts. Despite the exaggeration and florid colouring there is considerable artistic merit in the designs which are a vast improvement on the old timebills and posters which were nothing but an eyesore. A year ago the NER Company offered a prize to their servants for the best design for a poster and this brought forth a number of interesting exhibits which displayed considerable ability. I feel sure there is much latent artistic talent amongst the NER employees that only needs to be encouraged and once it were cultivated and fostered there might be no necessity for the Advertising and Publicity Department to go outside their own ranks for designs for advertising the attractions of the district".

Had the NER Company taken up this suggestion seriously the evolution of the poster, in the North East at least, would have been set back a number of years and the LNER poster would probably not have reached its peak before the outbreak of the Second World War in 1939. Fortunately the NER Company was already employing reputable artists such as Frank H. Mason, Fred Taylor and F. W. Booty in the early years of this century.

E. M. Horsley, the NER Advertising Manager, died in 1920. He had been responsible for considerable improvements and modernisation of his department and his restraint and good taste had gained for the NER a high reputation in the advertising world. G. W. J. Potter, a renowned railway author, paid a great tribute to Horsley – "Through Mr Horsley's excellent taste and original ideas the NER had attained a commanding lead in advertising literature, especially in artistic posters, there being no other company that could show such a varied and beautiful series of picture posters".

W. M. Teasdale, who had been the Trade Advertising Agent for the NER, succeeded Horsley as Advertising Manager. Within the short space of three years he had made his mark on railway advertising as it was said of him, in 1923, that he had made the LNER poster 'something different'.

Holiday Handbook
1937 by Frank Newbould

Each year the LNER produced a Holiday Handbook. It contained lists of hotels and guesthouses, suggestions of places to visit and advertisements. New resorts were featured as well as popular old ones. They were the original travel agent's brochures. The very earliest ones were produced by Thomas Cook, Bradshaw and W. H. Smith, whose original kiosks began on railway stations.

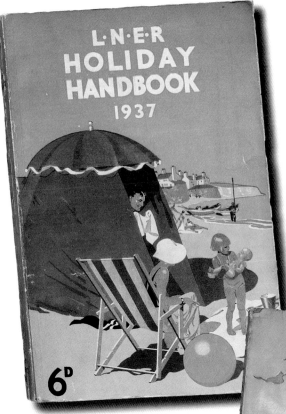

Holiday Handbook
1938 by Frank Newbould

Frank Newbould was born in Bradford, Yorkshire and studied at Bradford College of Art and at Camberwell School of Art. His attitude to his work was very practical. He believed that the artist should visit the location to be advertised for an hour or two to absorb the atmosphere and character of the place. He was also adamant that the artist should not draw from memory, as there was sure to be something that he would miss.

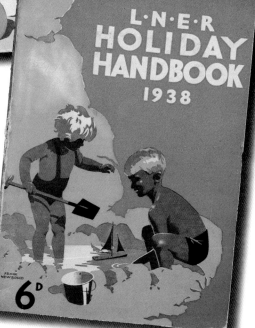

LNER Guide Books

The LNER produced elaborate illustrated guidebooks to encourage passengers to travel. These varied from Holiday Handbooks to Streamlined Services on named trains. Although they were produced for a single season and were ephemeral, many have survived and are beautifully illustrated. They also tell us a lot about how the LNER saw itself and its passengers. Railway travel provided a new kind of leisure activity, creating opportunities to sample the pleasure of cities, spend a day at the seaside or in the country or to attend a variety of sporting, cultural or social events. The railways soon realised that they could increase custom and boost their income by putting on extra trains for special excursions and holidays. This led to a whole new sphere of advertising in the shape of booklets and brochures. The LNER went on to publish numerous handbills and brochures to tempt the public to travel. This is a small selection.

**LNER Holiday Handbook
1939 by Michael**
A classic 1930s bathing belle looks optimistically towards a summer that was to be interrupted by the start of the Second World War.

**Holiday Handbook
1940 by J.F.**
'Fitness Wins' was a film directed by Mary Field in 1940. During the war the government funded films for the war effort. It covered subjects such as rationing, agricultural production, physical education and hygiene. Mary Field went on to work in children's education for the Rank Organisation. Health and fitness is here cleverly twinned with the East Coast sunshine.

The Eastern Belle Pullman Limited 1932
This train ran from London, Liverpool Street Station to Cromer, Yarmouth, Skegness, Hunstanton and Aldeburgh. The locomotive is a Great Northern Railway 2-8-0 currently on display at The National Railway Museum in York.

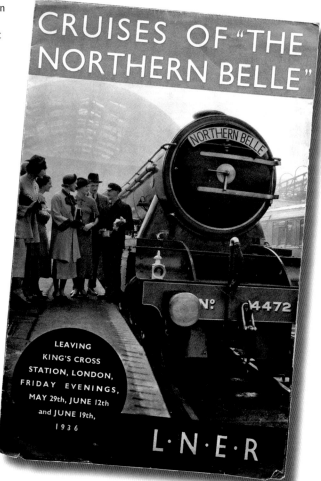

Cruises of 'The Northern Belle'
1936
The idea of the 'Land Cruise' was introduced by the LNER in 1933 with the cruising train 'The Northern Belle'. It was adapted from the fashionable pastime of liner cruising. June was the cruising month. 'The Northern Belle' left King's Cross Station at 9pm on a Friday evening for a 2000 mile tour and returned at 10.45am the following Friday. The fare was £20.00 and it carried 60 passengers. It carried 27 staff who had their own quarters and a 'host' to see to every whim of the passengers.

It saw itself as a self-contained first class hotel on wheels. The sleeping cars had air conditioning and electrically heated water was provided in each cabin with baths and showers.

There was also a lounge, saloon, writing room, ladies room, hairdressing salon and shop. The first stop after King's Cross was Barnard Castle in Northumberland.

**LNER Weekend Cruises to
The Continent
c1925**
The steamer SS Vienna was built for
the Great Eastern Railway in 1894 and
sailed from Harwick to Zeebrugge with
the LNER until it was scrapped in 1930
when a new vessel was built and the
name re-used.

WEEK-END CRUISES TO THE CONTINENT

L·N·E·R

No. 50

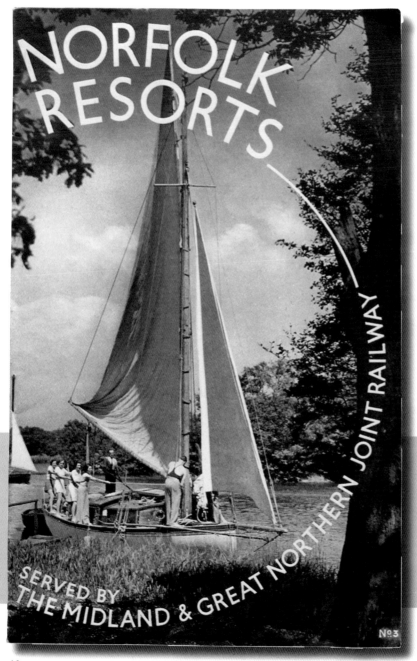

NORFOLK RESORTS

SERVED BY THE MIDLAND & GREAT NORTHERN JOINT RAILWAY

No3

Midland and Great Northern Joint Railway Norfolk Resorts c1935
The M & GN Railway was jointly owned by the LMS and LNER. It was fondly known as the Poppy Line. This leaflet was produced to promote holidays on the Broads and Fens of Norfolk.

Luggage Labels
Hotel luggage labels date from the late 1870s. Most of the LNERs had a sepia and white line drawing of the hotel like these two.

Be Early
By Tom Purvis 1932
This poster was produced to promote the company's new handbook for holidays on England's East Coast. The poster shows an illustration of the proverb 'the early bird catches the worm'. Pre-booked holidays and train tickets meant reliable profit for the LNER.

SCARBOROUGH

It's Quicker by Rail.

Holiday Guide to North East England
By V. L. Danvers c1935
No. 3 in a series of six. This is Bamburgh Castle, perched on a basalt outcrop of rock on the edge of the North Sea in Northumberland.

HOLIDAY GUIDE TO NORTH-EAST ENGLAND

No. 3

Scarborough
It's Quicker by Rail c1935
A very stylised view of the North Beach in Edwardian Scarborough when it was an upmarket resort known as the 'Queen of watering holes', superimposed with a late 1930s view of an A4 streamlined pacific and its fashionable travellers.

Excursions to Holland, Belgium and Germany via Harwich-Flushing
By A. Mouron Cassandre c1935
A stylised Art Deco design. Cassandre designs appeared to be incredibly simple but were highly evocative and complex. With its bold geometric shapes, Art Deco reflected and responded to the new industrial culture of the 1930s. Cassandre's work reflected the fast changing world he was living in. He conveys a sense of the new technology in his suggestion of movement and speed. You also get a vivid impression of the overwhelming size of the locomotive and steamer.

An LNER Menu card
By Verney L. Danvers c1925
Braemar Castle is in the Cairngorms on Royal Deeside. In its heyday many famous people passed through Ballater Station including many Royals travelling to and from Balmoral Castle.

An LNER Menu card
By Verney L. Danvers c1925
Showing the Yorkshire seaside town of Whitby.

'On Either Side'
by Frank Newbould c1935
The LNER was the first company to produce booklets for travellers to point out the sights and attractions *en route* between the larger cities. This practice has been revived in the twenty first century by Virgin Trains with their 'Window Gazer' guides.

ON EITHER SIDE

FEATURES OF INTEREST SEEN FROM THE TRAIN
BETWEEN
LONDON
(LIVERPOOL ST) &
EAST
ANGLIA

FRANK
NEWBOULD

LONDON & NORTH EASTERN RAILWAY

Camping Holidays
By Tom Purvis 1938
Another brochure to promote camping coaches. This shows a family enjoying a night campfire and singsong.

Camping Holidays
By Frank Newbould 1936
This brochure included information about campsites, youth hostels and camping coaches. The first LNER camping coaches were ten old Great Northern six-wheeler carriages placed beside LNER branch lines in 1933. From 1935 they were repainted in green and cream. The first ones were in Yorkshire, Cumberland and Westmoreland. The coach had a living room, kitchen, toilet and six sleeping compartments each with its own washbasin and running water supply. The campers were responsible for their own provisions.

**Camping Coaches in England and Scotland
By Tom Purvis c1938**
A poster version of the 1938
brochure cover.

George Stephenson
1925

George Stephenson, the founder of the railways built the first commercial railway in 1825. The Stockton and Darlington Railway was the first freight railway. Four years later in 1829 his locomotive *Rocket* won the Rainhill trials competition which gave him and his son, Robert, the contract to build all the locomotives for the first passenger railway: The Liverpool and Manchester Railway which opened in 1930. The LNER was keen to stress that the man who began the railways in Britain was from the North East. The others only followed.

Season Tickets on the LNER
1928

The LNER introduced new kinds of tickets and promotions to sell different types of tickets to different types of travellers. These two posters are to promote 'season tickets'. This cartoon shows a commuter walking purposefully towards his waiting train, with his season ticket, avoiding all the other passengers and queues. A season ticket could be bought in advance for less money that the number of journeys it covered would have cost on a daily basis. To us it seems normal but it was the LNER who invented the concept with advertising slogans such as "save time and money" and "pay less and travel more".

**The Travelling Eye – Advertising Space
By Herrick 1930**
The LNER even used its advertising
hoardings to sell advertising space to
other commercial companies. This art
deco design uses an eye to convey the
idea that advertising on the railway
network was like a moving advert. It
would be seen by more people than a
usual static hoarding.

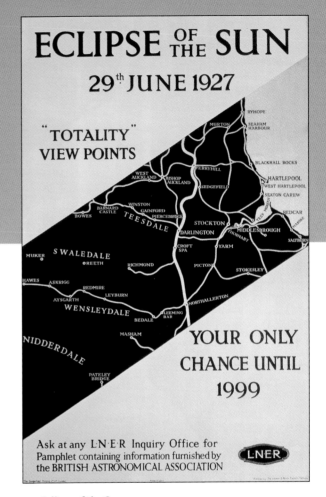

Eclipse of the Sun
The total eclipse of the sun in 1927 could be seen from both
LMS and LNER lines but both companies, naturally,
emphasised that the best views could be seen from their
lines – special trains were run to promote rail travel to North
Eastern England. 'Totality' is when the sun is totally
obscured by the moon and there is complete darkness. It
lasted for half a minute in the UK in 1927. About 3 million
people flocked north in what was believed to be the largest
ever single movement of people by train. The 1999 eclipse
has since been and gone. The best place to see it was
Cornwall and those who travelled almost all went by car.

The Silver Jubilee
By Frank Newbould 1935

In 1935 the LNER introduced the first streamline train in Britain which ran between London and Newcastle. This train with its own locomotives and carriages was highly distinctive and extremely popular. It generated an enormous amount of publicity material. *The Silver Jubilee* was usually pulled by one of Sir Nigel Gresley's A4 locomotives. Here it is pulled by *Silver Link*.

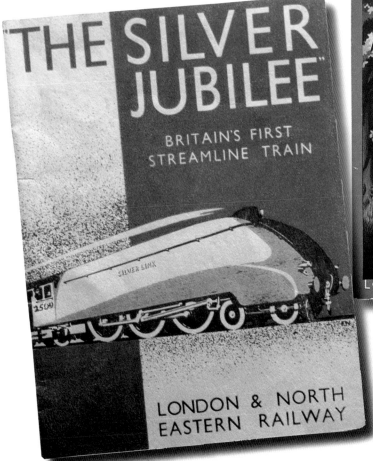

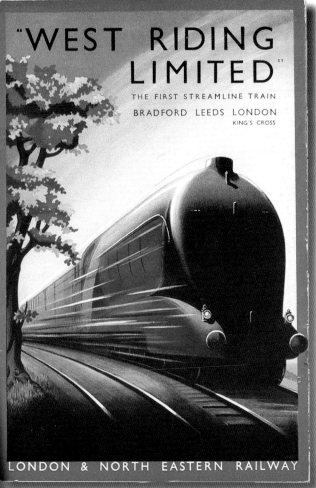

West Riding Limited
By Shep 1938

On this booklet cover three years later 'West Riding Limited' is also claimed to be the first streamline train. The locomotive shown is an A4 designed by Sir Nigel Gresley and may be *Mallard*. it was in this year that it broke the world steam speed record by travelling at 126mph.

Express Ease
By George Harrison c1924
The elegant Harrogate Pullman ran between King's Cross and Ripon. Harrogate was an important spa town and a centre of commerce during this time.

During the 1930s posters increasingly stressed the comfort of rail travel. Dining whilst travelling was not unusual, and the more prestigious trains boasted all-electric kitchens with both set and *a la carte* menus. The wine list on such trains as the *West Riding Limited*, the *Coronation* and the *Flying Scotsman* would disgrace a restaurant today. In 1938 the *West Riding Limited* offered no fewer than five different kinds of champagne and nine brands of mineral water!

The Coronation
By Frank Mason 1938
The Coronation ran between London and Edinburgh in six hours and was another luxury passenger express which ran on the East Coast route. Here it is just passing Berwick – the islands in the distance are the Farne Islands and Holy Island. The artist, Frank Mason, was a marine artist who designed railway posters for the North Eastern Railway, the LNER and British Railways (Eastern Region).

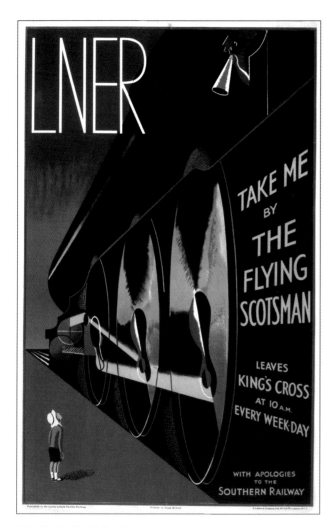

Take Me By The Flying Scotsman
By A. R. Thomson 1932

A caricature of the famous Southern Railway 'little boy' poster that poked fun at the Southern's homely style. The LNER wanted to project a very different image – it considered itself to be more professional. However, for all its artistic merits, this poster was not as popular with the public as the Southern one and was not re-issued.

What makes it more interesting is that the artist, A. R. Thompson, was profoundly deaf so the megaphone is very apt.

The Flying Scotsman – A Smart Turn Out
By Curtis Moffat c1935

The *Flying Scotsman* service ran from King's Cross from the 1870s first pulled by *The Sterling Single* on the North British Railway. The service continued throughout LNER and into BR days. The GNER still promotes the passenger express trains which run between King's Cross and Edinburgh as 'the route of the Flying Scotsman'. Here we see this famous Express train in the 1930s.

Olympic Games, Amsterdam
By A van Anrooy

In 1928 the LNER produced this poster to encourage travel to the Olympic Games in Amsterdam. The 1928 Olympic Games were the first to feature women's athletics and introduced the tradition of carrying the Olympic flame from Athens to the games.

The artist, Anton van Anrooy, was born in Holland but moved to London and became a naturalised British Citizen.

Innsbruck via Harwich
By Austin Cooper c1930
The LNER services from Harwich to the Continent ran by day and night to compete with the Southern Railway's night boat train.

New Rheingold Express
By Frank Newbould 1928

The *Rheingold* express ran from May 1928 until September 1939 from Harwich to Basel and Luzern; its Pullman coaches were not used after the war. The *Rheingold* was the only luxury German train comparable with the Wagon Lits Company. The English were the pioneers of tourism in Switzerland, especially the Swiss Alps where there were numerous good hotels with splendid mountain views.

Munich and Central Europe
By Ludwig Hohlwein 1929
This poster was produced to promote the LNER's services to Munich and other destinations in central Europe via Harwich. This shows the Fravenkirche in Munich's Central Square.
Ludwig Hohlwein first studied as an architect, which is reflected in his superb sense of layout and visual balance. He designed travel and commercial posters as well as political posters, including works for the Nazis during the Second World War. He died at Berchtesgaden in 1949.

East Coast Types
No. 5 The Deck-chair man
By Frank Newbould 1931

This was one of a series of six posters called 'East Coast Types' showing people who worked on the East Coast. This is the man who hired out the deck chairs to holidaymakers on the beach. The others were:

1. The Broads ferryman who drove the ferry.
2. The Scottish fisher lass who gutted the fish.
3. The lobster man who caught the lobsters.
4. The Scottish fishwife who smoked the fish.
6. The donkey boy who gave rides on the donkeys.

Skegness is so Bracing

By Frank Newbould after John Hassall 1933

The 'Jolly Fisherman' poster 'Skegness is So Bracing' is arguably the most famous English holiday poster. It was first published in 1908 by the Great Northern Railway which paid the artist twelve pounds for it. Since then, the 'Jolly Fisherman' has been caricatured over and over again and re-drawn many times. Even at its time it was an outstanding poster – most Edwardian and Victorian posters were restrained and factual. The 'Skegness is So Bracing' slogan is believed to have been the idea of Mr Hiley, the Chief Passenger Agent for the Great Northern Railway. The 'Jolly Fisherman' is still promoting Skegness as the ideal holiday resort; 2008 marks his centenary. John Hassall, however, died in relative obscurity in 1948.

Yorkshire Coast
By Stephen Bone 1933
The 'Summer Visitor' is a small child discovering a tidal rock pool on one of the sandy beaches of the Yorkshire Coast. The 'coastal residents' are the crabs, anemones, small fish and barnacles who live in the rock pool. A clever poster designed to make parents take their family on a seaside holiday. At this time most of the small Yorkshire seaside villages such as Robin Hood's Bay, Filey, Redcar, Saltburn and Whitby would have had their own railway stations.

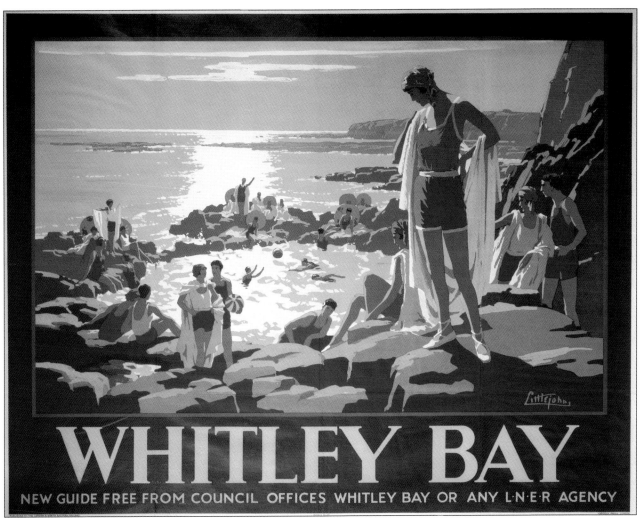

Whitley Bay
By John Littlejohns 1929
Originally a small fishing village, Whitley Bay
became a popular holiday resort in the 1930s.
Here we see night bathing.

FILEY **FOR THE FAMILY**

Illustrated booklet free from Council Offices
Filey Yorks or any L·N·E·R Enquiry Office

Filey for the Family
By Charles Pears 1924

Filey was a small fishing and farming village until the 18th Century when holiday visitors from Scarborough came to Filey for peace and quiet. The first railway opened in Filey in 1848 – by this time it was a fashionable holiday resort. It was later to see the opening of a Butlins holiday resort in 1947.

Here we see Filey Brigg. It is gritstone protruding out to the sea for nearly a mile forming a natural pier and breakwater.

Mablethorpe and Sutton-on-Sea
By Tom Purvis 1927
This poster was withdrawn soon after publication. The LNER received an angry letter from the Secretary of the Society for the Prevention of Cruelty to Animals, protesting that a picture of a child hanging on to a donkey's tail was an incentive to cruelty and, consequently, a harmful influence on the young.

East Coast Resorts
By Tom Purvis c1935
Tom Purvis was probably the greatest Railway Poster designer. This is typical of Purvis's style using flat primary colours and the elimination of detail to convey the seaside atmosphere of the era. It epitomises the youthful, carefree, fun of a 1930s seaside holiday.

CLACTON-ON-SEA
IT'S QUICKER BY RAIL
FOR ILLUSTRATED GUIDE APPLY, ENCLOSING 1d. STAMP TO :-
ROOM S.P. TOWN HALL, CLACTON-ON-SEA, OR OBTAINABLE FREE FROM L·N·E·R OFFICES AND AGENCIES

Clacton-on-Sea
By W. Smithson Broadhead c1930
In 1881 Clacton-on-Sea had a population of 651. By 1911 it was just under 10,000 due to the coming of the railway. Clacton had a sandy beach and warm climate and was an ideal holiday resort. The pier opened in 1871 and the branch line in 1882. The pier was widened in 1931 and a casino and pool added in 1932. It opened a Butlins holiday camp in 1938.

TOM PURVIS

EAST COAST BY L·N·E·R

East Coast – The Bath of Psyche
By Tom Purvis c1935
The child and dog playing in the water at the seaside is titled 'The Bath of Psyche'. This refers to the painting of the same name by Frederic Lord Leighton painted in 1890 which depicts the classical myth of Psyche and Cupid.

Purvis is mocking high classical and fine art by giving a railway poster the same title. He strongly believed that commercial art was as worth while as fine art and wrote several lectures and papers explaining why.

East Coast Joys 1931
By Tom Purvis
This was a series of six posters which form a continuous scene when placed next to each other, but each poster is so designed that it can also stand alone.

NO 3 SAFE SANDS

EAST COAST JOYS
travel by L·N·E·R
TO THE DRIER SIDE OF BRITAIN

NO 4 SEA BATHING

EAST COAST JOYS
travel by L·N·E·R
TO THE DRIER SIDE OF BRITAIN

East Coast Joys 1931
By Tom Purvis
This spread shows the other four posters in the same series.

Nº 5 SEA FISHING

EAST COAST JOYS
travel by L·N·E·R
TO THE DRIER SIDE OF BRITAIN

Nº6 SEA SPORTS

EAST COAST JOYS
travel by L·N·E·R
TO THE DRIER SIDE OF BRITAIN

The Golfers' Hotel

CRUDEN BAY HOTEL
ABERDEENSHIRE

OWNED AND MANAGED BY
THE LONDON AND NORTH EASTERN RAILWAY

FOR PARTICULARS OF TARIFFS APPLY RESIDENT MANAGER

Cruden Bay Hotel, Aberdeenshire
By Gordon Nicoll 1931

The Great North of Scotland Railway opened Cruden Bay Hotel and Golf Course in 1899. Under the auspices of the LNER, Cruden Bay was widely promoted. Inclusive fare excursions were available from Aberdeen, but fewer golfers than expected were attracted and in 1932 the service to Cruden Bay was withdrawn. In 1939 the hotel was requisitioned as an army hospital. It was handed back in 1945 and sold for demolition two years later. Perhaps Cruden Bay was too far for English golfers to travel when Gleneagles and St Andrews were on the way, or perhaps the golfing season was too short and there were no other real attractions – whatever the reason, Cruden Bay was a flop.

Gordon Nicoll (1888–1959) was a landscape painter and a member of the London Sketch Club. This poster is one of a series he designed on railway hotels for the LNER.

St Andrews

By H. G. Gawthorn c1930

From being almost exclusively a Scottish game for more than four hundred years, golf was adopted by the English in the nineteenth century. It had always been a traditional seaside game: the coastal turf and natural sand bunkers made for wonderful golfing country. As the game spread, there was an increasing demand by the growing middle classes for playing facilities. The railway companies saw possibilities of passengers and profit in this. Trains could transport golfers from the grime of the city to the coastal resorts, and although at first a bag of golf clubs and its owner on a railway station platform aroused curiosity, it soon became a familiar sight.

St Andrews, in Fife, Scotland is the home of the Royal and Ancient Golf Club and the LNER was quick to recognise it as a tourist magnet. It arranged for special golfers' tickets to be printed and organised holiday tours to the town.

Zetland Hotel, Saltburn
c1935

An unusual photomontage showing black and white views of the Zetland Hotel in Saltburn. Saltburn was considered to be one of the finest early Victorian planned seaside resorts. The railway was extended from Redcar to Saltburn in 1861 and was the most modern and up to date resort on the East Coast in its day. The hotel is now residential flats.

North Berwick
By Andrew Johnson c1935
The North Berwick Golf Club is a true links course laid out on a raised beach of brown sand varying between 10 and 30 feet above sea level.
The ladies section was added in 1934. From 1924 a through Sleeper Service ran from King's Cross to North Berwick for golfers and The Royal Hotel was built to accommodate them. North Berwick was advertised as the 'Biarritz of the North'.

Norfolk Broads
By V. L. Danvers 1925

This was one of a series of three posters advertising The Norfolk Broads. The Broads are a series of shallow lakes in the eastern part of England surrounded by reedy marshes and abounding with waterfowl, extending around the rivers Waveney and Yale.

The second – 'Try a fly' – shows fish leaping and the third shows ducks. These are, appropriately, Mallards. Sir Nigel Gresley, the engineer behind the A4 Locomotive *Mallard*, was a keen bird spotter and named several locomotives after bird species.

The artist Verney Danvers was influenced by Japanese art.

Try A Fly
By V. L. Danvers 1925

Fly fishing was a popular sport and holiday posters and brochures were published to encourage anglers to holiday at popular fishing spots such as the Yorkshire Dales, Malham Tarn and Scottish Rivers such as the Tay, Spey and Tweed.

The railways played a crucial role in the development of river fishing in the UK and the more affluent began to venture abroad to the salmon rivers of Norway. One of the benefits of the industrial revolution as far as anglers were concerned was that it provided them with a convenient means of travel – by the latter half of the 19th Century urban workers were taking advantage of the cheap, reliable travel offered by the railways.

As early as the 1870s angling clubs in the London area were negotiating successfully for cheap rail travel concessions for groups of anglers.

North East Coast Exhibition
By Septimus Scott 1929
The North East Coast Exhibition was promoted by Newcastle-upon-Tyne as a response to the economic depression, intended both to revive trade and lift morale. It provided a showcase for the industries of the North East, attracting over four million visitors. It had its own amusement park, stadium and flower gardens, and even an African village where over a hundred Senegalese natives lived their everyday lives in mud huts for the benefit of visitors. Among the famous products that made their first appearance there were Smith's Crisps and Newcastle Exhibition Ale. The LNER had its own display and set up an information pavilion in the exhibition grounds.

   The artist was Septimus Scott who was a poster artist, illustrator and the seventh son of his father.

The George Bennie Railplane System of Transport
By W. C. N. 1929

The George Bennie Railplane System of Transport was a suspended monorail for passengers, set above the existing railway. Thus passenger and freight traffic was separated. The passenger cars could be either propeller-driven or electrically powered. The project, set up at Milngavie, Scotland, as an experiment, was criticised by railway traction engineers. It was funded largely by George Bennie's own considerable income, and failed because it was carelessly planned, badly conceived and took no account of technical or economic factors. George Bennie had no formal engineering education and would not take advice from those who did. The projects he devised were largely unrealistic and included proposals to build a line between Damascus and Baghdad and a route over the Sahara! He had personal assets of over £120,000 in the 1930s but was penniless by 1957 when he died. The structure for the Railplane system was dismantled in 1956.

THE FORTH BRIDGE
ON THE
LONDON AND NORTH EASTERN RAILWAY OF ENGLAND AND SCOTLAND

The Forth Bridge
By H G Gawthorn 1929
The Forth Bridge crosses the estuary of the River Forth in Scotland to connect the East Coast route between London and Aberdeen. It was designed by Sir John Fowler and Sir Benjamin Baker and opened by the Prince of Wales in 1890. The man in the bottom left hand corner is the artist, Henry Gawthorn.

This poster, referring to the London and North Eastern Railway of England and Scotland, was probably designed for the American tourist market.

Yorkshire Moors
By Tom Purvis c1925
Rambling, or walking in the countryside, was a popular, relatively cheap and healthy way of using leisure time in between the wars. The LNER realised that some of the most delightful rambling spots could be reached from the major towns and cities by travelling to local stations and published rambling guides and tickets.

Ripon
By Charles Ginner 1936
The Cathedral of Ripon and the nearby 'Fountains Abbey' were advertised as places to visit in this historic inland resort. Ripon did not become a cathedral city until 1836 when the diocese of Ripon was created. This poster was commissioned in 1936 to celebrate this centenary. The artist, Charles Ginner, was born in France and moved to London in 1910 to join Sickert's Camden Town Group. He painted towns and landscapes.

To York – Dick Turpin's Ride
By Doris Zinkeisen 1934
The fact that Dick Turpin died nearly two hundred years before this poster was printed, that he never saw a railway line or locomotive and that he never travelled to York on his horse Black Bess, was irrelevant to the LNER's advertising department. The myth of the courageous highwayman riding from London to York in record time to escape capture and establish an alibi for himself was sufficiently powerful to be used to persuade potential travellers to visit York by train. It was also sufficiently well known to need no explanation. The figure of Dick Turpin astride his horse with York Minster in the background was all that was needed to recall the story. Dick Turpin was not the romantic 'Robin Hood' character that legend has made him. He was an unscrupulous thief. Richard Turpin was born in 1705 in Hemel Hempstead, where his father was the landlord of the Bell Inn. After leaving school at 16 he was apprenticed as a butcher and eventually set up his own shop. However, he could not cover his drinking and gambling debts and took to crime including highway robbery. To avoid capture he moved to Welton in East Yorkshire in 1737. He was convicted as the infamous highwayman whilst in prison and tried at York Assizes. He was hanged at York Tyburn on Tadcaster Road in 1739.

DICK TURPIN'S RIDE

TO YORK
TRAVEL BY TRAIN
FULL INFORMATION FROM L·N·E·R OFFICES & AGENCIES

PUBLISHED BY THE LONDON & NORTH EASTERN RAILWAY   PRINTED IN ENGLAND   CHORLEY & PICKERSGILL LTD LITHOGRAPHERS LEEDS

Harrogate
By Tom Purvis 1935
Harrogate was the inland resort par excellence. It had been a popular spa resort before the railways but it doubled its number of visitors after the first line was opened to the town in 1849. It boasted the "most handsomely appointed bathing establishments in Great Britain" where facilities included "natural sulphur water baths, needle baths, hot and cold douches, inhalation rooms and every modern method with latest improved appliances".

This poster shows 'bright young things' playing tennis in the park with the pavilion in the background. Notice Tom Purvis's use of elimination to give the feel of simple pleasure and fun.

HARROGATE

IT'S QUICKER BY RAIL

FREE GUIDE FROM F. J. C. BROOME, ROYAL BATHS, HARROGATE, OR ANY L·N·E·R OFFICE OR AGENCY

Harrogate
By Michael 1935
This second poster shows a similar group of people by night outside one of the grand hotels. The resort of Harrogate was always for the wealthy and it even had its own Pullman Service train once a day to and from King's Cross.

When Agatha Christie went missing in the 1920s it was rumoured that she went to a hotel in Harrogate.

KNARESBOROUGH

IT'S QUICKER BY RAIL

GUIDE FREE FROM COUNCIL OFFICE OR ANY L·N·E·R AGENCY

Knaresborough
By H G Gawthorn 1928

This and the poster opposite both use the technique of showing the resort from the train. The viewer sees what the passenger sees through the window.

The artist, Henry Gawthorn, was a Hitchcock like figure who put himself in most of his posters. Here he is holding his pipe and wearing a pince-nez looking down from Knaresborough Viaduct on to the River Nidd and the sleepy town of Knaresborough. He often has a panama hat, walking stick, striped blazer and black Labrador dog or any combination of these. He was also well known to the LNER lithographic printers for being a stickler for detail and not the easiest of men to work with.

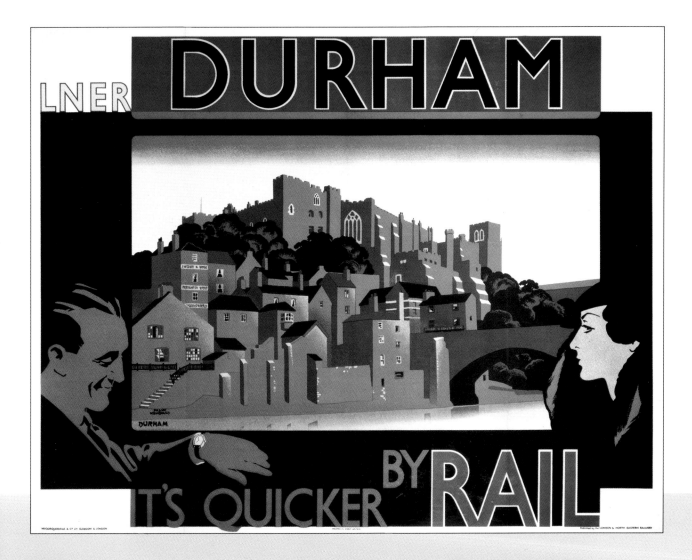

Durham
By Frank Newbould 1935
The cathedral City of Durham with its river, castle and medieval streets is promoted as a weekend break. The artist, Frank Newbould, actually went to all the places he was commissioned to advertise for the LNER and designed posters which epitomised the destination. The message is very simple – 'it's quicker by rail' and more comfortable. The gentleman is looking at his watch as the express train, probably from King's Cross, draws into the station.

St PAUL'S CATHEDRAL   By JAMES BATEMAN A.R.A.

LONDON
IT'S QUICKER BY RAIL
FULL INFORMATION FROM ANY L·N·E·R OFFICE OR AGENCY

St Paul's Cathedral
By James Bateman 1939

The LNER did not only promote seaside resorts but wanted to encourage travellers to visit 'inland resorts'. London was not just a business city but a place to visit for day-trippers and holidays from the provinces. As early as the 1920s the railway companies were advertising abroad to encourage Europeans and Americans to visit Britain and travel by train.

Whilst transport in London was largely served by London Transport, it was still the responsibility of the provincial railway companies to carry the visitor from the rest of Britain. The LNER ran from major city stations into King's Cross.

Here we see the hustle and bustle of the area around St Paul's with red London buses, a London policeman and city gentlemen.

Piccadilly Circus
By Fred Taylor 1925
Piccadilly Circus by night is shown in a very early LNER poster.
The LNER monogram used here was only used until 1927.
Notice the early omnibus and ladies' attire.

Factories on LNER Lines
By Austin Cooper c1930

The LNER promoted freight and trade custom as well as tourism and commuter passenger traffic. Freight revenue was an important part of the company's profit. Factories, railhead distribution and exceptional loads were encouraged. Machinery, engineering products, aggregates, minerals and metals that were too bulky or too heavy to be carried on ordinary goods wagons and vans were carried on special chassis. The LNER even offered its services as an industrial agent. There was a huge freight office based at King's Cross.

Britain's Coal
By George Bissill 1926

The LNER served the coal mining communities of north and south Yorkshire and whilst it used much of the coal for its own locomotive fuel it also delivered to power stations and docks. This poster was published in 1926 during the general strike to promote morale and to break the strike. Here we see healthy, strong miners at a coalface of a colliery served by the LNER.

Capacity/Mobility on the LNER
By H. G. Gawthorn 1932
Railway posters are usually associated with holidays but the LNER was keen to promote its freight services. Here we see a busy Manchester goods depot.

Power and Progress on the LNER
By H. G. Gawthorn 1929
Constructed in the 1920s the Sidings at Whitemoor on the Spalding line in
Lincolnshire were the largest in England.

The electric control box was one of the most important and modern on
the railway network.